THE POWER PILLARS

THE POWER PILLARS

Embrace the Principles to Mastering Your Life

Brenda Oriedi

Strategic Book Publishing
www.sbpra.net

For information about special discounts for bulk purchases, please contact Strategic Book Publishing, Special Sales, at bookorder@sbpra.net.

ISBN: 978-1-68235-371-4

ACKNOWLEDGEMENTS

I want to begin by offering my deepest gratitude to God, the source of all wisdom and inspiration. Your guidance and grace have been the cornerstone of my journey, and I am endlessly thankful for the wisdom You have bestowed upon me.

To my cherished Oriedi family: Your unwavering pride in my endeavours has been a constant source of motivation. Your love and support have been the wind beneath my wings, and I am eternally grateful for each one of you.

To my King: Thank you for always having my back and believing not just in me but in all my gifts. You continue to support me to make my dreams come true and I'm blessed to share them with you on this journey called life!

To my church family at Shekinah Shur Ministries, Nottingham: Thank you for nurturing my spiritual growth over the past two decades. Your teachings, prayers, and fellowship have enriched my life in countless ways, and I am blessed to be a part of this faith community.

To my sisters, (1.0 and 2.0): You have always been my number one supporter. Your encouragement, love, and belief in me have been my pillars of strength. I couldn't have asked for better sisters, and I am thankful for the bond we share.

To my publishers: Your dedication to bringing my work to life and your belief in my message have been invaluable. Your professionalism and commitment have made this journey possible, and I am grateful for your partnership.

To my readers: You are the heart and soul of this book. Your interest, feedback, and enthusiasm for my words have been a driving force behind my writing. I write with you in mind, and I am humbled by your support.

Lastly, to all those who choose to live in power: May your lives be filled with purpose, strength, and the realisation of your true potential. Together, we can make a positive impact on the world.

Thank you, from the depths of my heart, for being a part of this incredible journey.

With profound appreciation!

DEDICATION

For Dad: I know you would have been proud!
This is my promise that I won't stop putting your
name on books! I love you forever!

For Tricia, Kimberley, and Sidione:
Thank you for not permitting me to give up and
pushing me to finish this book! I love you guys!

CONTENTS

PROLOGUE: DEFINING THE NOTION OF POWER

Power as a noun is usually defined as the "capacity to act or perform; the ability to do or complete something." It speaks of competence in fulfilling or being. Power is the capacity to lead, regulate, or influence the actions of others and ultimately our own self.

Looking at the Bible as a whole is necessary to comprehend the idea of power according to biblical teachings. The Bible uses the word "power" in a variety of contexts, thus comprehending it requires examining how it is employed. Power is frequently viewed in the Old Testament as a manifestation of divine favour and is employed to carry out God's will; while in the New Testament it is viewed as a spiritual gift that is used to advance God's kingdom and spread the gospel. Power is never viewed as something to be misused or abused, but rather as something to be respected and used for the greater benefit. In the end, power is viewed as a tool to accomplish God's will, and not an end to its own self.

It would be a shame for us to wield power for others but fail on how we manage and regulate it our own self. Depending on the goals of the person using it, power can be utilised for both good and evil. Power is ultimately a tool that may be utilised to influence the environment we reside in. This has a lot to do with knowing, belief, and understanding but also exercising that which is known, believed, and understood in a way that creates the expected outcome or desire. Power we can see is influence, authority, jurisdiction, and leadership, but my favourite is responsibility! This God-given gift is a privilege as not only does it allows us the authority, but when handled well, can bring us to great harvest.

According to Matthew 28:18 in the New Testament, *"And Jesus came and said to them, 'All power in heaven and on earth has been given to me.'"* This chapter emphasises Jesus's authority and power and serves as an illustration of how power should be used constructively. The Bible also contains instructions on how to use authority in a way that benefits others, such as Ephesians 5:21, which says, *"Submitting yourselves one to another in the fear of God."* This text exhorts us to exercise our authority in a way that respects and benefits others. In the end, it's critical to keep in mind that all authority derives from God and should be applied to the responsibly.

Power, according to the Bible, is the capacity to bring about or sway change. Power is viewed as a gift from God and is frequently used for the good and service of others. The Bible views power as a good force that is used to do good and exalt God. *"I pray that the eyes of your heart may be enlightened,"* Ephesians 1:18-19 says, *"so that you may know the hope to which he has called you, the richness of his glorious inheritance in his holy people, and his incomparably great power for us who believe."* Here, power is characterised as a priceless gift from God to be put to good use.

God, as our Creator, has endowed us with a multifaceted power that encompasses the capacity to act, lead, regulate, and influence. Knowing how to use power to influence self and drive people, groups, and/ or organisations is essential to understanding power. Effective harnessing requires these three components of power, which can be interpreted in terms of influence, authority, and control. Influence is the capacity to persuade or persuade others to do something; and while control is the capacity to steer behaviour and resources, authority is the legal capacity to decide and enforce laws.

This divine empowerment is manifested in several ways:

1. **Free Will**: This is our God-given power to make choices and decisions. This free will allows us to act in accordance with our beliefs and values, shaping our lives and impacting the world around us.

2. **Moral and Spiritual Authority**: God has entrusted to us the power to live a life governed by moral and spiritual principles through His teachings and commandments. Our ability to control our thoughts, acts, and behaviours in accordance with His divine norms is made possible by this authority.

3. **Influence**: God's love and grace equips us to influence others through acts of compassion, kindness, and empathy. By demonstrating His love, we as his children can inspire positive change and uplift those around us.

4. **Stewardship of Creation**: We been given the authority to control and look after the environment since we are the Earth's stewards. This duty gives us the power to control the resources that have been made available to us, ensuring their sustainable use for future generations.

5. **Creativity and Innovation**: God's gift of creativity empowers us to innovate, create, and bring new ideas to life. This power to envision and shape the world around us reflects His divine creativity and invites us to contribute positively to society.

6. **Interpersonal Relationships**: We have the power to influence others through our relationships, interactions, and communication. By embodying love, respect, and understanding, we can lead by example and inspire those around us.

7. **Spiritual Transformation**: God's grace enables us to transform spiritually, moving from a state of brokenness to one of wholeness. This power to experience inner healing and growth allows us to influence others by sharing our testimony and journey.

8. **Prayer and Connection:** The power of prayer grants us a direct line of communication with God. Through prayer, we can seek guidance, invoke His intervention, and influence outcomes by aligning our desires with His divine will.

As kingdom children, God's power has been woven into the fabric of our existence, granting us the ability to act purposefully, lead with integrity, regulate our lives, and positively influence the world. This divine empowerment invites us to steward our gifts responsibly, fostering a harmonious relationship with God, fellow humans, and the world He has entrusted to our care.

This is the gift God has endowed upon us in the name of Jesus, and this is what gives us access to use and affect change here on earth and in our lives. This book is about helping us to understand and know how to correctly administer power in the different ways and areas of our lives but also how the importance of harnessing correctly can upgrade our thinking, sight, and overall walk with God. This means the application must fast be started with us. We must master how we handle power inherently and then find the biblical ways to translate that into our sphere of influence.

1. THE POWER OF ACCEPTANCE

The power of acceptance encompasses an individual's capacity to actively embrace, lead, regulate, and influence their own thoughts, emotions, and responses towards situations, people, or circumstances. It involves the ability to acknowledge and accommodate various perspectives, ideas, and realities, while guiding one's actions and influencing personal growth. By exercising this power, individuals can navigate challenges, shape their reactions, and influence their overall well-being by embracing circumstances with a balanced and constructive mindset.

From God's perspective, the power of acceptance is a transformative force that can bring peace and healing to our lives. Acceptance means acknowledging our flaws, weaknesses, and limitations, and surrendering them to God's will. It means recognising that we are not perfect, and that we need God's grace and mercy to guide us on our journey. When we accept ourselves and our circumstances, we open ourselves up to the possibility of growth and transformation. We become more resilient, compassionate, and empathetic, and we are better able to serve God and others. The power in acceptance is like a key to living a life of joy, purpose, and fulfilment, as we seek to align our will with God's will.

Acceptance, however, is not easy and often very challenging, if we track the lives of those in the Bible: From Abraham who was called to leave his family and later sacrifice his only son, or Jacob when he woke up next to Leah instead of Rachel, to his son Joseph who was sold into slavery by his brothers. Noah had to accept that no one believed him when he said rain was coming especially when they had never seen it before.

The Bible is full of challenges when it comes to acceptance that we can trace from the Old Testament all the way to New Testament with Mary and Joseph and, ultimately, Jesus who declared, "not my will but thine will be done" as he died to save us all. We all will, at one point or another, have to accept things about ourselves, our lives, others, and even God himself that we may find hard—to say the least—but must accept, especially if we believe in divine purpose and that the Creator knows what He intended for his creation better than we know ourselves.

Acceptance can be defined as:

1. The action of consenting to receive or undertake something offered.
2. The process or fact of being received as adequate, valid, or suitable.
3. Agreement with or belief in an idea or explanation.

Acceptance, as a law, can be seen as an express act or proposition by conduct that manifests the terms of an offer in a manner invited or required by the offer so that a binding contract is formed.

Eckhart Tolle defines acceptance as a "this is it" response to anything occurring in any moment of life. There, strength, peace, and serenity are available when one stops struggling to resist or hang on tightly to what is so in any given moment. What do I have right now? Now what am I experiencing? The point is, can one be sad when one is sad, afraid when afraid, silly when silly, happy when happy, judgmental when judgmental, overthinking when overthinking, serene when serene, etc. He goes on state that, "When we accept what is, it becomes possible to find freedom in the here and now."

Psychotherapist Russell Harris simplifies this by stating, "acceptance means allowing; allowing unwanted private experiences (thoughts, feelings, and urges) to come and go without struggling with them."

Beliefs and acceptance overlap in meaning. The acceptance of one's beliefs is important to show commitment and structure of one's life. Not only is it vital for survival, but it is used in everyday relationships. Acceptance in human psychology is a person's assent to the reality of a situation, recognising a process or condition (often a negative or uncomfortable situation) without attempting to change it or protest it.

The concept is close in meaning to *acquiescence*, (to find rest in). Acquiescence is something that believers can find in God. When we "rest in him," we in fact are trusting that God, in His supremacy, is able to do that which we ask and essentially cannot achieve without him. Psalms 4:8 states, *"In peace I will lie down and sleep, for you alone, LORD, make me dwell in safety."*

For those of us who walk with God, at some point in our journey, God will call or ask us to accept what we:

- Cannot understand, fathom, or change
- Do not see, looks impossible, or have never experienced
- Have experienced and seen but don't like
- What is contrary to what you know, want, or see
- What seems uncertain in terms of time
- Life events (what happened/past/history/mistakes)
- Loss/failures/pain/imperfections/brokenness
- Help from those we may not want to
- Dreams that seem farfetched
- Who you are/your story/accept others and their stories
- What you deserve/opportunities/worth/love/hope/grace/standards

As a starting point, I believe acceptance begins with awareness. This is what gives it power, but awareness calls for humility. Nothing begins until we accept, but you cannot accept without submission. Letting go of your control, opinions, rights, wants, desires, and trusting that what God is calling you to accept is for your good. You have to humble yourself to die to your own mind and ways. Humility always requires strength. The ability to lay down, to surrender, to trust, and to be vulnerable. There lies in the beginning of your "power."

The truth is, if we don't accept who we are and our journey so far, we reflect that back in our choices, habits, and relationships. Acceptance, when we hone it, it brings about light. Light in this instance is understanding, vision, clarity, and wisdom. When light shines, you will see what needs to be done. This is the power of acceptance.

* Acceptance removes false layers.
* Acceptance is the key to open doors, either new or old.
* Acceptance shifts perspective.
* By acceptance, scales are removed.
* Acceptance leads to clarity.
* Acceptance makes you own up and makes you accountable.
* It takes away validating of rebellion.
* Acceptance can only be embraced with courage.
* You must accept what you know as such; it highlights gaps in knowledge.
* When you're in a place of acceptance, you have a clearer view of what God is doing and working in your life. You look less at you and more at Him.
* Acceptance allows for you to see your reality for what it really is.
* Acceptance is the prerequisite to change; for in order to change, you must first accept.

* Acceptance doesn't always begin with understanding; however, the act itself always leads to revelation.
* Acceptance grants you the ability to manage yourself by giving you the choice to put yourself under subjection.
* Acceptance brings freedom.
* Acceptance is where your will dies and wherever your will dies, God takes over.

What Acceptance Is	What Acceptance Isn't
• Choice	• Fear
• Act	• Control
• Conscious and present awareness	• Logic
• Willingness	• Opinion
• Death of self	• Discussion
• Separation of will	• Manipulation to fit your desires
• Surrender	• Settling
• Submission	• Mediocrity
• Process	• False contentment
• Belief	• Rebellion
• Truth	• Opposition
• Humility	• Foolishness
• Understanding/ comprehension	• Unwillingness
• Knowledge	• Pride
• Faith	
• Sight/vision	
• Hope	

Sometimes acceptance is as simple as looking at the reality you face and saying, "Okay!" No resistance, no fighting, just plain taking it in stride; but how do we put the power of acceptance into effective practice? Here are a few steps that will lead us to yield this power and begin our transformation:

1. **Identify**: what do you need to accept?
2. **Understand** your vantage point: This is your position and the pace that you're operating in. I am here but need to get there and will need to do this to achieve that!
3. Be **honest** and get accountable. Ask yourself the hard questions, do I REALLY want the change? What am I willing to give up/do?
4. Develop **awareness** of the "why" that has led to where you are, including recognising limits/influences, choices, and so on.
5. **Submit** to the challenge that is ahead of you.
6. **Surrender** your will and trust God.

Acceptance is a concept that can be difficult to embrace, particularly when we are faced with circumstances that challenge our beliefs or expectations. However, from a spiritual perspective, acceptance is a crucial component of our relationship with God. Here are some additional thoughts to consider on the transformative power of acceptance:

- Acceptance doesn't mean complacency or resignation. Rather, it's about acknowledging reality as it is, rather than as we wish it were.

This can be a difficult process, but it allows us to move forward with greater clarity and purpose.

- Acceptance is an act of trust in God. When we surrender our flaws, weaknesses, and limitations to God's will, we are acknowledging that we trust in His plan for our lives. This can be a deeply comforting and freeing experience, as we let go of the burden of trying to control everything ourselves.

- Acceptance opens the door to growth and transformation. When we stop resisting what is, we create space for new possibilities to emerge. We become more open to learning, more receptive to feedback, and more willing to take risks.

- Acceptance is a path to greater compassion and empathy. When we accept ourselves and others as imperfect beings, we are better able to extend grace and understanding to those around us. This can deepen our relationships and help us to connect more authentically with others.

Ultimately, acceptance is a key to living a life of peace and fulfilment. When we align our will with God's will, we tap into a source of wisdom and guidance that can help us navigate the challenges of life with greater ease and grace. We can experience a sense of purpose and joy that transcends our circumstances and brings us closer to the divine.

2. THE POWER OF ALLIANCE

The power of alliance refers to the capacity of individuals or groups to come together, collaborate, and collectively act, lead, regulate, and influence outcomes. It involves the ability to form partnerships, coalitions, or associations with shared goals, where members combine their strengths and resources to achieve common objectives. Through alliances, entities can exert greater influence, regulate their efforts, and lead initiatives that might be challenging to accomplish individually, thereby amplifying their impact and achieving collective success.

Being in alliance means having a formal agreement or partnership between two or more parties to achieve a common goal or objective. In your day-to-day relationship with God, this alliance is formed through prayer and obedience. If you have not realised, there is power in agreement. This means there is one who is always for you and works in your favour despite all that may be happening around you. Alliances are not only formed with God but in all our other relationships too.

The Tower of Babel story, found in Genesis 11:1-9, begins with humanity coming together with a shared goal: to build a tower that reaches the heavens. This cooperation among people can be seen as an illustration of the immense power that comes with alliances. When individuals or groups unite toward a common purpose, they can achieve remarkable feats. In this case, the people of Babel, through their unity, were attempting to defy the limits of human achievement and reach a divine level. This underscores the potential and ambition inherent in collaborative efforts.

Alliances can take many diverse forms, contingent on the needs and goals of the parties involved such as:

- **Military alliances:** These are made when countries agree to work together to defend themselves against a common enemy. Examples of military alliances include NATO and the Warsaw Pact.
- **Business alliances**: These are formed between companies in order to gain a competitive advantage in the market. Examples of business alliances include joint ventures and strategic partnerships.
- **Political alliances:** These are formed between political parties or groups in order to achieve a common goal, such as winning an election or passing a piece of legislation.

They say that it's not always what you know, but rather, who you know. Connections are powerful and can be keys to doors and places of great influence. Connections can also be our downfall if we are allied with the enemies of our destinies, so choose your connection very carefully. In his book, *Relational Intelligence*, Dr Dharius Daniels states: "part of our purpose is to be a relational asset—not a liability—" So as much as it is important for us who we connect with, we must assess ourselves and find out if we are the type of people others should be allied with. We must bear in mind our character and dispositions in relation with others and determine if others can rely on us. Are we good soil? Can people invest in us and us in them for a greater return?

In the Bible it is clear that God choose to not only be in association with the children of Israel but that through Christ, He united those of us who are gentiles unto Himself. He chose us and said, *"I call you my own"* (Isaiah 43). We trace this alliance in the different books, and we can see clearly what the consequences are when the children of Israel disassociated themselves from God. God is a covenant-keeping God, which means His deals last a lifetime. They supersede generations and time and when He is connected with you, He does not break His covenant, realising this is where your power will come from. It's in the knowing of who you are allied with, not just knowing what the terms and conditions of the covenant are, but more so why they were established. And for God, it is simple ... just read John 3:16.

Let me reiterate, it is always in your best interest to work with God than against Him. Amos 3:3 asks a profound question: *"Can two walk together, except they be agreed?"* We walk the earth, completely ignoring its creator in our choices and decisions and wonder why we struggle as such. We ignore His voice and wonder why we stumble, why the path takes forty years instead of forty days? Agreement in prayer with God, can bring healing and restoration to relationships, families, and communities and aligns us with the will of God and inviting His presence into our midst.

The power of agreement can also extend beyond our immediate circle of influence, but it's important to remember that agreement in prayer does not mean we will always get what we want. Rather, it means that we are submitting our desires and requests to God's will and trusting that He knows what is best for us.

Over the last year, I have experienced God move me from one season to the next. These seasons seem to have crept upon me without warning. Some seasons broke me strategically like pins inserted into every nerve ending of my body, while others had me feeling like a tossed ship in the middle of a storm with no clue where the horizon is. I felt like I was subjugated with loss from each end and just before I was able to lift my head and breathe, something else happened. In the midst of these seasons, certain core topics would arise to teach me a lesson here and another there. One thing that I have learnt is God doesn't not need to ask for permission to fulfil His purpose when there is a word over your life. The Bible says, *"Heaven and earth will pass away, but my words shall not pass away"* (Matthew 24:35). If you are one who submits or wants to submit your will to His, this is the first and most important lesson for you to comprehend. God will do exactly what He said he will do. Jonah taught us that being an ally of

God, goes along way than being in opposition to Him. These seasons that I felt like God was against me, was Him essentially using my life to fulfil His word.

God will do what God wants to do and He does not need our permission. What the Holy Spirit taught me is what God requires is our cooperation. That is the key ingredient in whether you are working with or against the plan of God in your life. It is actually easy to identify if God is working or not. How do you know you may ask? Because when God is working in your life, it doesn't feel comfortable, it doesn't feel relevant, and it definitely doesn't feel right. I am not sure why, but I realised that it's easy to miss the hand of God especially during our rough seasons and maybe it's to do with our expectations. We never seem to expect God to be in the midst of the stormy days; truth is we will be asking him to quiet the storm or rescue us not realising that He actually may be the storm. Are we just conditioned to deal with just a "little" trouble, but when the heat gets hotter, we want God to rescue us?—because "It definitely couldn't be God why I'm going through so much!" we mutter.

When we apply a negative perception to our situation, forgetting that "his ways are not our ways," we will be quick to ask for the rescue, not realising that those are the same seasons that He may using to elevate, develop, and make us if we would only cooperate. Believe me, not all "trouble" is from the Lord, but if you are submitted to His will, He will use what was meant to break you, to make you and give you the victory.

My experiences taught me that there is power when we harness the right attitude and insight. There are certain key lessons that take a lot to learn, comprehend, and, even more so, apply, but when we do, the outcome is always worth it. In order to understand the concept of power in its core, it's imperative to have true insight about what God calls "power" and how we can harness it in some core areas in our lives in order to walk in the way in which He has called us to walk especially when it comes to agreeing with heaven! The essence of this lies in Matthew 18:19 that states: *"If two of you shall agree on earth as touching anything that they shall ask, it shall be done for them of my Father which is in heaven."*

The Bible demonstrates that even from the beginning of time at the start of creation, the Father, the Son, and the Holy Spirit are always in one accord. The scriptures are filled with endless encounters of what happens when we are in unity and in one accord with God; we see the sun stand still for Joshua, or fire come down from heaven for Elisha, the rock produce water and seas part for the Israelites, and the donkey speaks all to fulfil God's agenda and purpose. And when we agree with heaven we are told, *"Whatsoever we bind on earth, is bound in heaven and whatsoever we lose on earth, is loosed in heaven."* This is the power of being allied with the right connection. I urge you today to submit your will, let go, and allow God to work our His perfect plan for you. Therein lies your power for it allows you access to the authority that is in Heaven to use here on earth!! Remember, it is ALWAYS in your best interest to work with God, for if God be for you, who can be against you? (Romans 8:31).

3. THE POWER OF CULTIVATION

The power of cultivation encompasses the capacity to take purposeful actions to nurture, develop, and refine various aspects of oneself, others, or the environment. It involves leading efforts to foster growth and improvement, regulating the processes of development, and influencing positive change through deliberate and systematic actions. By wielding the power of cultivation, individuals can act to enhance skills, relationships, or conditions, guiding the journey towards progress and success, while also influencing the outcomes and influencing the direction of growth and advancement.

The word *cultivation* refers to preparation that comes before the planting/growing. In agriculture, it is the ability of humans to intentionally and systematically grow plants and animals for their own benefit. This power has been a significant contributor to human progress and civilization, allowing for the development of agriculture, which in turn has led to the establishment of permanent settlements, the creation of surplus food supplies, and the growth of complex societies. Cultivation has also had a profound impact on the environment, affecting everything from soil quality to the spread of invasive species. Despite its many benefits, the power of cultivation also carries with its certain risks and responsibilities, including the need to balance the needs of people with those of the natural world, and to ensure that the benefits of cultivation are distributed fairly and equitably.

This principle of cultivation can be paralleled in our relationships with oneself, God and with others in that it involves nurturing and growing relationships over time. In the context of our relationship with God, this means taking intentional steps to deepen our understanding of Him and draw closer to Him. Remember, there is always a preparation before the planting and/or the growing. This might involve regular prayer and Bible study, attending worship services, fasting, serving others in our gifts and other spiritual disciplines.

God views the power of cultivation as an essential tool for personal growth and spiritual development. Throughout the Bible, we see examples of individuals who cultivated their relationship with God through prayer, meditation, and worship. In fact, Jesus himself frequently withdrew to quiet places to pray and be alone with God.

The importance of cultivating our own relationship with God cannot be overstated. It is through this relationship that we find peace, strength, and guidance in our lives. When we cultivate our relationship with God, we become more attuned to his will and are better equipped to handle the challenges and struggles that come our way.

There are many ways to cultivate our relationship with God. One of the most important is through prayer. When we pray, we are communicating with God and opening ourselves up to his presence. We open regular dialogue with him and listen as he speaks back to us. As with any relationship, communicating well is essential to building intimacy and growth. We then extend this relationship as we know more about him and his ways, we start to practice that in our own lives by practicing gratitude, forgiveness, and compassion towards others.

There is power in cultivation. In the same way we toil to break soil, we must do the same to our souls so as to make sure we are good soil that we can bear much fruit. Cultivation is a vital tool for personal and spiritual growth. By intentionally cultivating our relationship with God, we can deepen our connection with him and find peace and strength in our lives and this in turn reflects in our relationship with others.

In our relationships with others, cultivation means investing time, energy and effort into building and maintaining strong connections. It calls for us to be intentional in developing and nurturing relationships with others over time. The benefits of cultivating relationships include building trust, creating mutual support systems, increasing feelings of belonging and connectedness, and potentially opening up new opportunities for personal and professional growth. We can do this by actively listening to others, showing empathy and understanding, and being present in their lives. It also means being intentional about resolving conflicts and working through challenges together.

The power of cultivation involves recognising that relationships are dynamic and require ongoing effort and attention. By prioritising these values in our relationships with God and others, we can create deeper, more meaningful connections that enrich our lives and bring us closer to those around us. Philippians 2:12, encourages by saying:

> *So then, my dear ones, just as you have always obeyed [my instructions with enthusiasm], not only in my presence, but now much more in my absence, continue to work out your salvation [that is, cultivate it, bring it to full effect, actively pursue spiritual maturity] with awe-inspired fear and trembling [using serious caution and critical self-evaluation to avoid anything that might offend God or discredit the name of Christ].*

Cultivating relationships takes time and effort, but it is a worthwhile investment in our personal and professional lives, because by investing in our connections with others, we can build trust, support, and a sense of belonging that enriches our lives in countless ways.

- Developing strong relationships requires active listening, empathy, and a willingness to be vulnerable with others. By taking the time to understand and support the people in our lives, we can build deeper connections and foster mutual growth.

- In a professional context, cultivating relationships can lead to new job opportunities, referrals, and partnerships. By networking and building a reputation as a trustworthy and reliable colleague, we can expand our career prospects and open up new doors for growth.
- Cultivating relationships also means being intentional about the people we choose to surround ourselves with. By seeking out relationships with those who share our values and goals, we can create a supportive and uplifting community that helps us achieve our dreams. Proverbs 11:14 highlights this by saying, *"Where there is no counsel, the people fall; But in the multitude of counsellors there is safety."*

In addition to the personal and professional benefits, cultivating relationships can also lead to improved physical and mental health. Studies have shown that having a strong support system can lower stress levels, reduce the risk of depression and anxiety, and even boost the immune system. If we surround ourselves with the right people, they will speak life over us. The word of God states in Proverbs 16:24: *"Gracious words are a honeycomb, sweet to the soul and healing to the bones."*

Building and maintaining relationships can also help us to extend our thinking and take in new knowledge. Connecting with others who have various backgrounds, experiences, and perspectives can help us learn new things and broaden our understanding of the world around us.

To continue to foster strong relationships, it's important to prioritise communication, listen actively, and be willing to compromise and work through conflicts. By doing so, we can continue to reap the benefits of meaningful connections with others.

In addition to prioritising communication, active listening, and conflict resolution, there are a few other ways to strengthen relationships with others especially with the help of the Holy Spirit who is our teacher here on earth, these include:

- **Giving Honour**: Letting others know how much we appreciate them can go a long way in strengthening our relationships. Whether it's a simple "thank you" or a heartfelt note of appreciation, taking the time to express gratitude can make others feel valued and deepen our connections with them. The Bible puts it like this: *"Render therefore to all their dues: tribute to whom tribute is due; custom to whom custom; fear to whom fear; honour to whom honour"* (Romans 13:7 KJV).

- **Restoration**: When others are going through a tough time, showing empathy can help them feel heard and supported. This can involve actively listening, offering words of comfort, or simply being present with them. Galatians 6:1(AMP) states: *"Brothers, if anyone is caught in any sin, you who are spiritual [that* *is, you who are responsive to the guidance of the Spirit] are to restore such a person in a spirit of gentleness [not with a sense of superiority or self-righteousness], keeping a watchful eye on yourself, so that you are not tempted as well."*

- **Coming Together**: While communication and conflict resolution are important, it's also important to come together! Whether it's trying a new activity, exploring a new place, or simply sharing a meal, worshipping together, making time for enjoyable experiences can help build positive memories and strengthen our relationships. Hebrews 10 24-25 says, *"And let us consider one another to provoke unto love and to good works: Not forsaking the assembling of ourselves together, as the manner of some is; but exhorting one another: and so much the more, as ye see the day approaching."* 1 Cor 1:10 expands on this and says, *"Now I entreat you, brethren, in the name of our Lord Jesus Christ, to cultivate a spirit of harmony—all of you—and that there be no divisions among you, but rather a perfect union through your having one mind and one judgement."*

By cultivating our relationships and our interactions with others, we can continue to foster strong, meaningful connections that bring joy and fulfilment to our lives.

4. THE POWER OF PERMISSION

The power of permission refers to the ability to grant or receive authorisation, lead others towards certain actions, regulate access to resources or opportunities, and influence the decisions or behaviours of individuals or groups within established boundaries. It involves the capacity to allow or enable specific actions, endeavours, or endeavours to occur, thereby guiding and influencing the course of events and interactions. Through this power, individuals or entities can shape outcomes and create an environment where certain actions are facilitated or restricted based on their influence and control over granting permission.

The power of permission is often underestimated, overlooked, and unappreciated, yet it holds a significant role in our lives. Permission is the act of allowing something to happen or granting someone the authority to do something. In many cases, it can be the difference between success and failure. When we receive permission, we often feel validated, seen, heard, and empowered, which in turn motivates us to act. Equally, when we are denied permission, it can lead to frustration and even resentment. This concept is a fascinating one and concept can be seen in many different aspects of life. At its core, it refers to the idea that we have the ability to choose what we do and how we act. This concept is closely tied to the idea of free will, which is the belief that we have the power to make choices that are not determined by fate, destiny, or any other external force.

The power of permission lies in its ability to create a sense of trust and respect between individuals, and to encourage collaboration and innovation. By giving permission, we give others the freedom to explore new ideas and take risks, ultimately leading to growth and progress. This is the same permission God gave us from the creation of the universe.

In the Bible, the idea of free will is closely tied to the concept of God giving us permission to make our own choices. For example, the story of Adam and Eve in the Garden of Eden is often used to illustrate this point. God told Adam and Eve that they could eat from any tree in the garden except for one. However, they chose to eat from that tree anyway, and as a result, they were expelled from the garden.

This story is often interpreted as a demonstration of the power of permission. God gave Adam and Eve permission to choose whether or not to eat from the forbidden tree, and they chose to exercise that freedom. This is evidence of the importance of free will, and it underscores the notion that we are responsible for our own actions.

Of course, the power of permission goes far beyond religious contexts. It is a fundamental aspect of being human, and it is something that we all must grapple with in our daily lives. We are constantly faced with choices, both big and small, and we must decide which path we will take. Sometimes these choices are easy, and sometimes they are difficult, but they are always ours to make.

For us as Christians, God is seen as the ultimate authority who has created everything and everyone. As such, we believe that God has given each individual the ability to make choices and decisions for themselves. However, this freedom is not absolute, and there are certain boundaries that individuals must respect. In this sense, God views permission in the lives of his creation as a necessary part of maintaining order and harmony in the world. When we as individuals seek permission and guidance from God, we are acknowledging our dependency on Him and recognising that we are not in control of everything. Ultimately, by following God's guidance and seeking his permission, we as individuals can live in accordance with his will and find meaning and purpose in our lives.

Overall, the power of permission lies in its ability to create a positive and empowering environment, where individuals feel supported and encouraged to take risks and pursue their goals. By recognising the importance of permission and using it wisely, we can unlock our full potential and achieve greater success and fulfilment in all areas of life.

It is, however, amazing how many of us never start or step out because we keep waiting for permission from others. The story of the twelve spies in Numbers 13, is a good example of a nation that had the permission from the almighty God to possess their promise land but allowed what they saw feed on their fears and as such, they influenced all but one.

Don't get me wrong, it's always good to consult but do not let the acceptance of others paralyse you to the point that you forfeit your dreams and ambitions. You are who you are because God created and determined you as such. His word says so, not me! *"I knew you before I formed you in your mother's womb. Before you were born, I set you apart and appointed you as my prophet to the nations"* (Jeremiah 1:5 NLT).

He goes on to say in Psalms 139:

You made all the delicate, inner parts of my body and knit me together in my mother's womb. Thank you for making me so wonderfully complex! Your workmanship is marvellous—how well I know it. You watched me as I was being formed in utter seclusion, as I was woven together in the dark of the womb. You saw me before I was born. Every day of my life was recorded in your book. Every moment was laid out before a single day had passed (Psalms 139:13

Remember, the power of permission is a reminder that we are in control of our own lives. We have the ability to make choices, and those choices have consequences. Whether we are making decisions about our careers, our relationships, or our personal lives, we must always remember that we have the power to choose our own path. We must also understand that as creations who are made in the image of God, if we yield this power with honour, we can change and support others and create a space or path where people are free to grow and start understanding who God created them to be.

The concept of the power of permission extends beyond religion and into many aspects of our daily lives. It reminds us that we have agency over the choices we make and the actions we take. Here are some ways in which the power of permission plays out in different areas of life:

- Giving employees the power of permission to make choices about their work can lead to greater job satisfaction and a stronger sense of ownership over their work. In the workplace, permission can be used to empower employees and promote creativity and innovation. By giving employees the authority to make decisions and try out new ideas, we can create a culture of trust and collaboration, which can lead to increased job satisfaction and productivity.

- In relationships, the power of permission can be a valuable tool for setting boundaries, building trust, and maintaining healthy communication. When partners feel that they have the power to say no, they are more likely to feel respected and valued in the relationship. By seeking and granting permission, we can avoid misunderstandings and conflicts, and foster open communication and mutual respect.

- In personal growth, the power of permission can be a powerful tool for overcoming limiting beliefs and achieving our goals. By giving ourselves permission to try new things and take risks, we can break out of old patterns and discover new possibilities for our lives.

The power of permission is a reminder that we have agency over our lives and the choices we make. It is up to each of us to use that power wisely and make choices that align with our values and goals. If we then submit this knowledge to the all-knowing God, we align ourselves more with His divine purpose than the agenda of others. Who then to understand you more than the creator? Who gets to determine how far you reach other than the one who numbers your days?

Remember, you are here as part of a master plan that even those around you cannot fathom. Do not let go of God and all that He has called you to be. It is time for you to BECOME! Even you yourself cannot fathom the plans He has for you. Let Him show you! Let Him direct your paths and let him be the lamp unto your feet. Believe me, He knows how the story ends. He is both the Author and the Finisher of your story!

So BECOME!! Begin to be! Grow to be! Develop into who He created you to be! ... YOU HAVE PERMISSION!

5. THE POWER OF DECISION

The power of decision pertains to an individual's capability to make choices, take actions, guide processes, and influence outcomes. It encompasses the ability to lead oneself or others through thoughtful and purposeful choices, regulating courses of action, and influencing the direction of events based on careful consideration and judgment. This power enables individuals to shape their own lives and the lives of those around them by determining the path they take and the impact they have on various aspects of life.

When it comes to harnessing the power of decision making, it is imperative that we are guided by faith. There is a profound impact of decision making in the context of our Christian faith. By delving into biblical examples and employing strategic approaches, we can learn to make decisions that align with God's will and purpose for our lives. We can navigate the complexity of life with faith, wisdom, and purpose by harnessing the power of decision-making through biblical insights and strategic techniques. We can learn to make decisions that please God and bring us closer to His divine purpose for our life by basing them on His Word, seeking godly counsel, giving up control, and placing importance on the leading of the Holy Spirit.

The issue remains, how do we know that the decision we have made is the right one? How are we to measure whether the course or the pathway we embark on when what we want to decide is actually going to keep us aligned with purpose? There are four different ways we can use to weigh the motives, understanding, and sometimes the impact of the decision.

1. Decisions Should be Shaped by God's Word

When contemplating a decision, it is important as a child of God to seek His voice, firstly in His word and those He has assigned as counsel in your life. We must learn to test the word, but more importantly know when God himself is speaking to us and sometimes through us.

In Exodus we read about Moses and how he struggled with God's choice to send him to deliver his people, and by Exodus 3:10-12 as we witness Moses's decision to heed God's call and lead the Israelites out of Egypt exemplifies the importance of aligning our decisions with God's Word. Just as Moses sought guidance in Scripture, we too can base our choices on the timeless truths found within the Bible.

Strategy: Scripture Study and Prayer

Our comprehension of God's nature and precepts is deepened by frequent Bible study and prayer, which empowers us to make faith-based decisions. We can more clearly understand God's will by looking to His Word for direction.

Delving deeper into the concept of making decisions shaped by God's Word, we can draw insights from different theological perspectives:

Biblical Interpretation: Various schools of biblical interpretation emphasise the importance of understanding the historical and cultural context of scripture especially during our studies. By delving into the original meanings of passages, we can extract principles that guide our decision making. For example, employing historical-grammatical interpretation can shed light on how biblical characters navigated choices, revealing lessons applicable to our lives today. Tools like the Strong's concordance and Bible dictionaries can assist in this.

Moral Theology: Moral theologians emphasise the role of ethics and virtues in decision making. Drawing from thinkers like Thomas Aquinas, we can integrate virtues like prudence, temperance, and justice into our choices. Decisions rooted in these virtues align with God's character and contribute to our spiritual growth.

2: The Wisdom of Seeking Counsel

If you have heard the saying "no man is an island," then the importance of counsel and surrounding yourself with the right people is a familiar concept. As stated in some of the above chapters, relationships matter from forming alliances to cultivating friendships, power lies in surrounding yourself in wise counsel and having accountability.

The early church's decision to seek counsel from leaders before making critical choices highlights the wisdom of seeking guidance from fellow believers. Just as they gathered to discuss and discern God's direction, we too can benefit from the perspectives of wise and faithful mentors (Acts 15:6-31).

Strategy: Seeking Godly Counsel

Cultivating relationships with mature believers provides a source of guidance and accountability. Through open conversations and seeking wise counsel, we can gain valuable insights that aid our decision-making process.

When studying the wisdom of pursuing counsel, we can assimilate insights from varied theological perspectives:

> **Ecclesiology**: The study of the church can shed light on the collective aspect of decision making. Understanding the role of the church community as the Body of Christ emphasises the importance of seeking input from fellow believers. Just as the early church sought counsel from apostolic leaders, we can tap into the collective wisdom of our kingdom community.

> **Relational Theology**: By embracing the idea of a relational God, we recognise that seeking

counsel reflects our desire to connect with others in meaningful ways. Just as the Triune God exists in perfect relationship, we are called to engage in relationships that nurture our spiritual journey. Seeking counsel becomes an illustration of our interdependence as members of the Body of Christ.

3. Surrendering Control and Trusting God

When we begin to acknowledge and perceive the voice of God, we will understand that one of the key things that comes with moving when God speaks is in the posture of surrender. In Abraham's Journey of Faith (Genesis 12:1-4), this is demonstrated as we witness Abraham's decision to leave his homeland and trust in God's promises and exemplifies the power of surrendering control and placing our trust in the Almighty. In the same way, our decisions can reflect a willingness to let go and follow God's lead. This is usually one of the hardest things, as we as humans love to control our outcomes. However, blind faith and trust in God calls for us to walk even if we don't know where we are going or see the next step.

Strategy: Cultivating a Trusting Heart

It is hard to trust who you don't know. Such is the state if you don't know who God is, you will struggle to trust him when he speaks. Developing a heart of trust involves surrendering our desires and plans to God and knowing that he loves us and his plans for us are good (Jeremiah

29:11). Through prayer and reflection, we can learn to submit our decisions to Him, allowing His will to guide our paths.

Exploring surrender and trust through different theological lenses can enhances our understanding on the cultivation of trust.

Process Theology: Emphasises God's interaction with creation and the dynamic nature of God's involvement in our lives. Surrendering control is not passive resignation but an active participation in the ongoing process of God's plan. Even in the face of uncertainty, trusting God entails aligning ourselves with His purpose.

Soteriology: The study of salvation reminds us that surrendering control is rooted in acknowledging our dependence on God's grace. Just as salvation is a gift we cannot earn, surrendering our decisions to God acknowledges that our efforts alone are insufficient. Trusting God's providence aligns with the understanding that He is the ultimate orchestrator of our lives.

4: The Impact of Decisions on Our Witness

Being true to yourself is such an important aspect on decision making. I always advise people and say, "Make a decision that you can live with!" We must always be aware on the impact of our decisions not only to others but to ourselves. We cannot afford certain choices to be based on somebody else's voice or opinion. As much as external forces are things we must consider, that internal voice we hear must also be listened to. There will always be external stimuli that come at us, but the impact to our witness we must not neglect. In Daniel 1:8-16, we see his resolve when dealing with Nebuchadnezzar. Daniel's decision to remain faithful to his convictions even in the face of adversity illustrates how our choices can impact our witness as Christians. Like Daniel, our decisions can reflect our commitment to living out our faith, even when it's challenging.

Strategy: Living Out Our Convictions

We can demonstrate God's transforming power in our lives by purposefully making choices that are consistent with our Christian principles. Our decisions can be a sign of our faith and lead people to Christ.

5: Surrendering Control and Trusting God

By assimilating theological insights, we might think about how choices affect our witness:

> **Missiology:** Missiologists highlight the role of believers as ambassadors of Christ, entrusted with the task of sharing the Gospel. Our decisions directly impact our ability to effectively communicate Christ's message. Just as missionaries adapt their behaviour to connect with different cultures, our decisions shape our witness to a diverse world.

Cultural Engagement: Engaging with cultural theology emphasises the relevance of Christianity in contemporary society. Our decisions reflect our engagement with cultural norms, and aligning our choices with Christ's teachings can bridge the gap between faith and culture. By making decisions that challenge societal norms in line with our faith, we demonstrate the transformative power of Christ in our lives.

Embracing the Challenge: The Importance of Making Tough Decisions

Learning to make decisions, especially when they are difficult, is a crucial aspect of our Christian journey. The Bible is full of believers who had to walk the rough road of tough decisions. It is through these challenges that we experience growth, deepen our faith, and reflect the character of Christ. Let's explore why it's essential to embrace the process of making hard decisions:

Spiritual Maturation: Just as physical muscles strengthen through resistance, our spiritual growth is nurtured by facing challenging decisions. My Pastor has a saying that "Trouble comes to ask you who you are!" Difficult choices provide opportunities to exercise our faith, patience, and reliance on God's guidance. Embracing these challenges leads to spiritual evolution, as we learn to navigate complexities with wisdom and discernment.

Alignment with God's Will: Making hard decisions often requires seeking God's will fervently. Wrestling with tough choices prompts us to draw closer to God in prayer and meditation. Through these struggles, we refine our ability to discern His voice and align our decisions with His perfect plan for our lives.

Character Development: The crucible of difficult decisions moulds our character, shaping us into individuals who mirror Christ's virtues. Just as Jesus exemplified courage, selflessness, and obedience in the face of the cross, we too can cultivate these traits through the choices we make. Hard decisions offer opportunities to exhibit Christ-like character even when the path is challenging.

Witness to Others: Our response to difficult decisions serves as a powerful witness to those around us. When we choose to rely on God's strength and guidance, even in the midst of adversity, we demonstrate the transformative power of faith. Others witness our resilience, trust, and unwavering commitment to God, inspiring them to seek a deeper relationship with Him. Although trials don't produce faith, they refine it and showcase it and its power.

Testimony of God's Faithfulness: Making tough decisions provides us with firsthand experiences of God's faithfulness. When we step out in obedience, even when it's difficult, we often witness His provision, guidance, and peace in remarkable ways. These testimonies become a wellspring of encouragement, reminding us and others of God's unwavering presence in challenging times.

Eternal Perspective: Embracing hard decisions through the lens of eternity shifts our focus from temporary discomfort to everlasting significance. Just as Paul declared that our present sufferings are not worth comparing to the glory that awaits us (Romans 8:18), difficult decisions become an opportunity to invest in the eternal Kingdom and participate in God's redemptive plan.

Learning to make decisions, especially when they are hard, is an integral part of our Christian pilgrimage. Through these challenges, we experience spiritual growth, align our choices with God's will, develop Christ-like character, bear witness to others, testify to God's faithfulness, and embrace an eternal perspective. By embracing the process of making tough decisions, we navigate life's uncertainties with unwavering faith, ultimately drawing closer to God and fulfilling our purpose as His disciples.

Navigating the Decision Making Process

Once we understand why we need to make decisions and can weigh the importance, the impact and sometimes even the cost of decisions, we begin to value the power that God has placed in us. As kingdom ambassadors, we see that there is so much power in decision making and sometimes we just need some practical steps to enable us to remain in the posture of serving God through our decisions.

Let us combine all that we have already discussed in this chapter and explore practical methods and/or steps that can help us in making choices that are consistent with God's will and purpose as we integrate the principles of our Christian faith and an understanding of why we make difficult decisions:

1. **Prayerful Reflection**: Begin by seeking God's guidance through prayer and reflection. Set aside dedicated time to commune with God, surrender your desires, and seek His wisdom. Invite the Holy Spirit to illuminate your thoughts and reveal insights as you consider the decision before you. Talk to him and make this a part of your everyday life and learn his voice and his ways.

2. **Scriptural Exploration:** Engage in a thorough study of relevant scriptures that offer guidance or insights related to your decision. Allow the Bible to provide foundational principles and examples that inform your understanding of God's perspective on the matter.

3. **Seeking Counsel:** Reach out to trusted mentors, pastors, or fellow believers who can offer

godly counsel. Share your thoughts, concerns, and uncertainties with them, inviting their insights and perspectives. Their wisdom can provide valuable clarity and a different viewpoint.

4. **Moral and Ethical Considerations:** Evaluate the decision's alignment with biblical ethics and virtues. Consider how your choice reflects principles such as love, integrity, justice, and compassion. Assess whether your decision will contribute positively to your character and witness.

5. **Practical Assessment:** Analyse the practical implications of your decision. Consider how it impacts your responsibilities, relationships, and commitments. Assess potential outcomes and consequences, keeping in mind both short-term and long-term effects.

6. **Inner Peace and Conviction**: Pay attention to your inner sense of peace and conviction. In alignment with Colossians 3:15, let the peace of Christ rule in your heart. If you feel a deep sense of peace and assurance about a particular direction, it may indicate God's leading.

7. **Surrender and Trust:** Surrender your preferences, fears, and concerns to God. Embrace a posture of trust, acknowledging that His ways are higher than ours (Isaiah 55:8-9). Release any need for control and commit to following His lead, even if it means stepping into the unknown.

8. **Waiting on God:** Be willing to wait patiently for God's timing and clarity. Just as Abraham waited for God's promise (Hebrews 6:15), allow yourself to wait for God's confirmation or direction if needed. Avoid rushing into decisions out of impatience or pressure.

9. **Fasting and Solemn Seeking:** In cases of particularly significant decisions, consider engaging in a period of fasting and dedicated seeking of God's will. Fasting can help you focus your heart and mind on God's voice and discernment.

10. **Accountability and Review:** Share your decision-making process and conclusion with an accountability partner or mentor. This step ensures that your choices are evaluated from an external perspective and aligned with your commitment to seeking God's will.

By embracing a deliberate and prayerful decision-making process that incorporates spiritual principles, biblical insights, trusted counsel, practical assessment, surrender, and patience, you can navigate choices with confidence and clarity. Through each step, you honour God's sovereignty and invite His guidance, leading to decisions that align with His will and purpose for your life. This is the way to not only harness the power of decision but to implement it daily in your life!

6. THE POWER OF UNDERSTANDING

The power of understanding refers to the capacity to comprehend, interpret, and empathise with different perspectives, ideas, or situations. It involves the ability to lead oneself or others through insightful comprehension, regulate emotional responses by gaining deeper insights, and influence interactions and decisions by fostering empathy and open-mindedness. This power allows individuals to act based on informed insights, guide discussions for clarity and cooperation, and influence relationships by demonstrating empathy and a genuine grasp of various viewpoints, thereby promoting harmonious interactions and constructive outcomes.

One of my favourite scriptures is Proverbs 4:7, which says, *"Wisdom is the principal thing; therefore, get wisdom: and with all thy getting get understanding."* The transformative power of understanding and why we should embrace divine wisdom is depicted in such a beautiful way in this verse because divine wisdom always calls for understanding.

There lies a profound power in understanding—a gift that allows us to decipher the intricacies of language, foster empathy, and navigate the complexities of human interaction. Through the lens of psychological, sociological, and spiritual perspectives, we explore why God's emphasis on acquiring understanding holds the key to transformative growth and harmonious relationships.

Understanding is the link that allows us to transform knowledge into wisdom. It involves the ability to discern patterns, perceive implications, and make connections that lead to wise choices and actions. Without understanding, knowledge remains fragmented and may not be applied effectively or wisely.

In a spiritual context, understanding deepens our comprehension of God's Word and His will. It allows us to connect biblical truths, discern spiritual insights, and apply wisdom in our daily lives. Seeking understanding aligns with the pursuit of both knowledge and wisdom, enriching our relationship with God and guiding us toward a life characterized by discernment, insight, and the application of divine truths.

The power of understanding is a force that unites individuals, cultures, and faiths. It embodies the essence of God's wisdom, inviting us to rise above surface-level knowledge and delve into the depths of empathy, discernment, and compassion. By heeding God's timeless counsel to "get understanding," we embark on a transformative journey that enriches our lives, enhances our relationships, and contributes to the flourishing of a harmonious and interconnected world.

The Essence of Understanding

Understanding is a cognitive and emotional process that bridges the gap between individuals, enabling comprehension and empathy. Delving into the essence of understanding reveals its significance in our lives:

Psychological Insight: Understanding is the cornerstone of effective communication, as it involves grasping both the content and context of messages. It fosters mutual respect and emotional connection by acknowledging diverse perspectives and experiences.

Societal Harmony: In a sociological context, understanding forms the basis for harmonious relationships within diverse communities. It promotes cultural empathy, tolerance, and the ability to coexist in a world enriched by various languages and traditions.

God's Emphasis on Acquiring Understanding

The wisdom of God's guidance in Proverbs 4:7, *"In all your getting, get understanding,"* reflects His desire for His creation to seek wisdom that transcends mere knowledge. Understanding aligns with His divine purpose for our lives:

Spiritual Discernment: In the spiritual realm, understanding deepens our discernment of God's will and character. It allows us to grasp the nuances of His Word, draw closer to His heart, and align our decisions with His desires.

Embracing His Image: Seeking understanding reflects our pursuit of mirroring God's nature, marked by His infinite wisdom and compassion. As we understand others, we honour the divine image they bear and foster unity amidst diversity.

Understanding in Practice

Applying the power of understanding requires intentional efforts and a transformation of heart and mind:

Active Empathy: Active empathy involves placing ourselves in others' shoes to comprehend their experiences, emotions, and perspectives. Just as Christ empathised with human suffering, we can empathise with others' journeys, fostering authentic connections.

Cultural Competence: Understanding across cultural boundaries necessitates cultural competence. By seeking to understand cultural norms, values, and communication styles, we transcend differences and cultivate genuine relationships.

Spiritual Growth: Seeking understanding in our spiritual walk involves delving into Scripture, engaging in prayerful meditation, and seeking godly counsel. This pursuit deepens our faith and equips us to discern God's voice amid life's complexities.

Conflict Resolution: Understanding is a potent tool for conflict resolution. By comprehending underlying motivations and emotions, we can address disagreements with empathy, grace, and a commitment to reconciliation.

The Transformational Impact of Understanding

The transformative power of understanding reverberates through individual growth, relational harmony, and a world enriched by empathy:

Personal Transformation: Understanding enriches our intellectual and emotional capacities. It cultivates humility, broadens perspectives, and fosters a willingness to learn and evolve.

Relational Enrichment: In relationships, understanding strengthens bonds, fosters trust, and promotes effective communication. It bridges gaps and cultivates a supportive environment where individuals can thrive.

Global Unity: Understanding transcends cultural, linguistic, and ideological barriers, nurturing global unity. By seeking understanding, we contribute to a world where empathy and compassion prevail over division.

Navigating God's Will Through Understanding

The relationship between understanding and God's will for our lives is a profound interplay that guides our decisions, shapes our character, and deepens our relationship with the Creator. As we seek to comprehend His desires and align our choices with His divine purpose, understanding becomes a crucial catalyst in navigating our spiritual journey; there is divine alignment through understanding.

Understanding aligns us by helping us discern God's voice. Understanding enhances our ability to discern God's voice amid the noise of life. By immersing ourselves in His Word and cultivating a heart of understanding, we become attuned to His leading, allowing us to make decisions that align with His will. This in turn will help us gain clarity amidst ambiguity. As we know, God's will may sometimes seem enigmatic, but seeking understanding allows us to unravel the layers of His plans. Just as Joseph interpreted dreams and Daniel understood visions, a heart grounded in understanding unveils the purpose behind life's complexities. Understanding also empowers us to make decisions that reflect God's wisdom. Proverbs 3:5-6 encourages us to trust in the Lord with all our hearts and lean not on our own understanding. Yet, seeking understanding enables us to make informed choices rooted in biblical principles.

We begin and sometimes continue to deepen our spiritual connection which grows our intimacy with God. As we seek to comprehend His heart and purpose, we draw closer to Him in prayer, worship, and study of the scripture. This intimate connection transforms our desires, aligning them with His. Once our intimacy with God grows and deepens, we find ourselves in surrender and obedience. Understanding God's will encourages our willingness to surrender our plans and desires in obedience. Just as Jesus understood His Father's will and submitted to the cross, our understanding prompts us to yield to His leading even when it requires sacrifice.

Pursuing understanding is a lifelong journey that mirrors God's desire for continuous growth in our relationship with Him. It encourages us to remain curious, humble, and open to His guidance as we seek to comprehend the depths of His purpose and His will for us. Just as Moses understood his role in leading the Israelites, and Paul comprehended his mission to the Gentiles, our understanding guides us to fulfil the specific purpose God has ordained for us. Understanding bolsters our faith as we witness the intersection of God's will and our obedience. It propels us to step out in faith, trusting that His plans are far greater than our limited perspective, and that He orchestrates all things for His glory. Understanding will lead us to want to always be in a space connected with God. Jesus emphasised that bearing fruit requires abiding in Him (John 15:4-5). Understanding God's will deepens our abiding, enabling us to bear the fruit of love, joy, peace, patience, kindness, goodness, faithfulness, gentleness, and self-control (Galatians 5:22-23).

The relationship between understanding and God's will for our lives is an intricate dance that encompasses discernment, intimacy, surrender, obedience, and fruitful living. As we cultivate a heart of understanding, we embark on a transformative journey that aligns our decisions with God's divine purpose. By seeking to comprehend His will, we embrace a life marked by wisdom, purpose, and a deepening connection with the One who holds the blueprint for our existence. Through understanding, we navigate the intricate tapestry of God's will, step by step, trusting in His guidance and surrendering to His perfect plan.

The Connection between Wisdom, Knowledge, and Understanding

Understanding, wisdom, and knowledge are interconnected concepts, each playing a distinct role in our cognitive and spiritual growth. While they are related, they encompass different aspects of our intellectual and spiritual development:

Knowledge:

Knowledge refers to the acquisition of information and facts. It involves the gathering of data, facts, and details about various subjects. Knowledge is obtained through learning, observation, study, and experience. It answers the "what" and "who" questions and provides the foundational facts that form the basis of understanding and wisdom.

Wisdom:

Wisdom goes beyond knowledge and involves the ability to apply knowledge in a discerning and meaningful way. It encompasses sound judgment, critical thinking, and the capacity to make wise decisions based on a deep understanding of situations and contexts. Wisdom is often gained through experience, reflection, and a mature perspective. It answers the "how" and "why" questions, guiding us in navigating complex situations and making choices that align with moral and ethical principles.

Understanding:

Understanding involves the ability to grasp the meaning, significance, and implications of information and concepts. It goes beyond mere knowledge by delving into the deeper layers of meaning and context. Understanding allows us to connect ideas, relate concepts, and see the interrelationships between various pieces of information. It involves insight and comprehension, enabling us to see the bigger picture and make connections that enhance our perspective.

Understanding serves as a bridge between knowledge and wisdom. While knowledge provides the raw material, understanding processes and synthesizes that knowledge into a coherent and insightful framework. This framework, in turn, forms the foundation for wisdom.

Knowledge → Understanding → Wisdom:

Knowledge is the accumulation of facts and information.

Understanding involves comprehending the meaning and context of that knowledge.

Wisdom applies understanding to make thoughtful and discerning decisions.

Exploring the Relationship between Understanding and Vision

Understanding has a profound impact on our vision, both in the literal and metaphorical sense. It shapes how we perceive the world, interpret information, make decisions, and navigate our spiritual and personal journeys. One thing that understanding brings to our vision is clarity and focus. Just as a lens focuses light to create a clear image, understanding sharpens our perception of situations, concepts, and truths. It removes the fog of confusion and helps us see things as they truly are. This in turn adds depth and nuance to our vision. It allows us to see beyond surface-level appearances and delve into the intricate layers of meaning and significance. Our vision becomes multidimensional, revealing hidden truths and connections.

Once we have clear focus and clarity, understanding provides a broader perspective and context. It enables us to see the bigger picture, recognizing how individual elements fit into a larger framework. This expanded vision helps us make more informed judgments and decisions. Our vision becomes attuned to identifying patterns, motives, and implications that may not be immediately apparent. This discernment is a key aspect of wisdom, guiding us in making thoughtful choices in our lives and those of others. Understanding others fosters empathy and connection. It enables us to see the world from their perspective, cultivating compassion and a deeper sense of shared humanity. This enriched vision enhances our relationships and interactions.

In a spiritual context, understanding shapes our vision of God, faith, and purpose. It allows us to perceive spiritual truths and insights that go beyond the physical realm. Our spiritual vision becomes attuned to divine revelations and eternal realities. This propels us forward towards growth and evolvement. It helps us envision possibilities, set goals, and create a roadmap for personal and spiritual growth. Our vision becomes a driving force that guides our aspirations and actions and uses understanding as a catalyst for transformation and change. As we gain insight and comprehension, our vision advances, and we become more open to change, adaptation, and continuous improvement.

Understanding aligns our vision with our values and beliefs and ensures that what we see and perceive resonates with our core principles, promoting authenticity and integrity in our actions. It helps us cultivate a vision grounded in an understanding that fosters resilience and hope. It allows us to navigate challenges with a sense of purpose and optimism, knowing that our insights and knowledge will guide us through adversity.

Understanding, in principle, sharpens our perception, broadens our viewpoint, and empowers us to engage with the world and our inner selves in meaningful and transforming ways. Understanding transforms our vision into a powerful tool for growth, connection, and positive change.

How to Measure Your Understanding

Measuring understanding, whether of God, oneself, or others, entails a complex evaluation that considers a variety of elements. Here are some important factors to consider:

1. **Depth of Insight:** Consider how deeply you can explain and describe the subject of understanding. Can you articulate the underlying concepts, principles, and nuances?
2. **Contextual Awareness:** Reflect on whether you understand how the subject fits within its broader context. This could involve understanding how a particular biblical passage relates to the entire Bible, how your own emotions relate to your life experiences, or how someone's actions reflect their cultural background.
3. **Application and Implications:** Evaluate your ability to apply your understanding to real-life situations. Can you take what you've understood and use it to make informed decisions or offer practical insights?
4. **Synthesis of Information**: Assess your capacity to connect different pieces of information or concepts. Can you integrate various aspects of your understanding to form a cohesive and comprehensive view?
5. **Empathy and Perspective-Taking:** Gauge your ability to empathise and consider oth-

er viewpoints. In the case of understanding others, can you see situations from their perspective, even if you don't personally agree?

6. **Reflective Self-Awareness**: For understanding oneself, consider how well you can introspect and recognise your own emotions, motivations, strengths, and weaknesses.

7. **Alignment with Values**: Examine whether your understanding aligns with your core values, beliefs, and principles. Is your understanding congruent with what you hold to be true and important?

8. **Openness to Growth**: Assess whether your understanding is fixed or if you're open to refining and expanding it based on new information or experiences.

9. **Consistency and Coherence**: For understanding God, consider if your understanding is consistent with the teachings and principles of your faith.

10. **Ability to Teach or Share**: An effective measure of understanding is your ability to teach or explain the subject matter to others in a clear and meaningful way.

11. **Impact on Behaviour and Decisions**: Evaluate whether your understanding influences your behaviour, choices, and interactions. Understanding should lead to practical changes and improved relationships.

12. **Lifelong Learning**: Acknowledge that understanding is a continuous process. Strive for

ongoing learning, growth, and deepening of your understanding over time.

Remember that understanding is not an all-or-nothing concept; it exists on a spectrum. The goal is not just to arrive at an understanding but to continuously engage in the process of learning, refining, and applying what you've learned in ways that enrich your spiritual, personal, and relational journey.

7. THE POWER OF PERSPECTIVE

The power of perspective refers to the ability of an individual to shape their understanding, interpretation, and outlook on various situations, ideas, or events. It encompasses the capacity to influence one's thoughts, emotions, and decisions, ultimately guiding how they interact with the world and others. This unique lens of perception enables individuals to lead, communicate, and navigate their surroundings effectively, thereby impacting their interactions and shaping their overall experiences.

Perception is more than sight. It goes further than what we see but more so how we hear, comprehend and even respond. Throughout the ages, both science and philosophy have grappled with the profound question of how we perceive the world. And while sight undoubtedly plays a crucial role, it is just one thread in the intricate fabric of perception. Our senses are a symphony of experiences, woven together to create a comprehensive understanding of our surroundings. To truly appreciate the depth and complexity of perception, we must embrace its transformative power and learn how to exercise it in our day-to-day lives.

The concept of perspective is so profound in how it shapes our understanding, influences our choices, and impacts our Christian journey. By exploring the definition of perspective and its profound effects on our vision, we unveil the power it holds in aligning our decisions with God's will and purpose.

Perspective can be defined as the unique lens through which we perceive and interpret the world around us. It is a combination of our experiences, beliefs, values, and emotions that colour our understanding of reality. Just as a painter uses perspective to create depth and dimension in art, we too wield this potent tool to shape our spiritual and practical landscapes.

The Bible reminds us that God's ways and thoughts are higher than ours (Isaiah 55:8-9). This acknowledgment of divine perspective emphasizes our need to seek His vantage point in order to make decisions that align with His will. As we walk through different seasons, our perspective needs to consider how God sees before we take a step. Divine perspective has a great influence on our vision, our world, how we interpret challenges, and how we navigate decisions.

We can transform our perspective by recognising its power and intentionally cultivating a perspective that enhances our decision-making and spiritual journey. Romans 12:2 encourages us to renew our minds. Engaging in regular Scripture study, prayer, and meditation allows us to align our perspective with God's truth and wisdom while adopting a perspective of gratitude helps us focus on God's blessings rather than dwelling on difficulties. Gratitude shifts our attention from what we lack to what God has graciously provided. Cultivating an eternal perspective reminds us that our decisions have lasting significance. When we prioritize the Kingdom of God, we make choices that resonate in eternity.

The power of perspective is woven into the fabric of our lives like an exquisite tapestry. We unleash the potential to align our decisions with God's will and purpose by grasping its definition and realising its enormous effects on our vision. We gain insight, wisdom, and the ability to perceive the world through the lens of faith via conscious attempts to shift our perspective, leading us to decisions that honour God and contribute to His redeeming plan.

Let's examine the far-reaching effects of perspective on our vision:

Interpretation of Events: Just as a prism refracts light into a spectrum of colours, our perspective can transform events into varying shades of meaning. An event that may appear discouraging from one angle can become a source of growth and opportunity when viewed through a lens of faith and trust in God's providence.

Response to Challenges: Perspective determines whether we view challenges as insurmountable obstacles or as opportunities for God to work miraculously. When we adopt a perspective rooted in God's promises, difficulties become stepping stones to spiritual maturity and deeper reliance on Him.

Decision-Making Framework: Our perspective shapes the criteria we use when making decisions. Decisions filtered through a lens of selflessness, compassion, and eternal impact align more closely with God's desires for our lives.

Attitude and Gratitude: A positive perspective leads to an attitude of gratitude. When we recognize the blessings amidst hardships, we cultivate a heart of thankfulness that transforms our outlook on life.

Alignment with God's Perspective: As we strive to emulate Christ, our perspective should align with His. Viewing circumstances through the lens of sacrificial love, humility, and the eternal Kingdom enables us to make choices that mirror Christ's character.

The Transformational Impact of Shifting Perspective in Faith and Godly Perception

The power of perspective extends beyond mere understanding; it has the remarkable ability to shape the very fabric of our faith life and our perception of God.

A shift in how we see things can lead to transformative outcomes that profoundly impact our spiritual journey and our relationship with our Creator.

As we deepen our trust and surrender with God, we inevitably begin shifting our perspective to allow us to view God as the sovereign orchestrator of our lives. As we relinquish the need for control and place our trust in His wisdom, we experience a deeper sense of surrender. Recognising that God's perspective encompasses a vast eternal plan reassures us that He works all things together for our good (Romans 8:28).

This change in perspective enables us to see challenges as opportunities for God's grace to shine. We move from a mindset of defeat to one of hope and perseverance. By focusing on God's faithfulness throughout history and His promises for our future, we find strength and courage to endure hardships with unwavering faith and embrace his blessings. God's blessings, however, sometimes come in a way that don't "look" like blessings. Shifting our perspective towards gratitude transforms how we perceive God's blessings. A heart that recognises every good gift as a manifestation of God's love leads to a constant attitude of thanksgiving. Gratitude shifts our focus from what we lack to the abundant blessings that surround us, nurturing a deeper appreciation for God's provision.

The power of perspective has a great impact on the revelation that comes when we want to unveil God's character and experience him in our lives. A change in perspective unveils facets of God's character that we might overlook. When we view Him not only as Creator but also as a loving Father, a faithful Shepherd, and a compassionate Saviour, our relationship with Him deepens. This newfound understanding prompts us to approach God with awe, reverence, and intimacy. Revelation allows us to walk in the different dispensations on his supremacy and grace and we begin to find joy beyond circumstances. As we perceive Him as a God who desires to reveal Himself to us, we actively seek His presence through prayer, meditation, and Scripture study. This newfound intimacy enriches our faith life and strengthens our spiritual walk. The temporal challenges of life fade in light of the eternal glory that awaits. This shift leads to a joy that remains unshaken by trials, as we set our eyes on the imperishable rewards of a life lived for God. The minute we start viewing ourselves as instruments of God's grace, we transform our understanding of service. When we recognise that God's perspective identifies us as co-laborers in His Kingdom, we are empowered to serve with purpose and impact. Our actions become a reflection of His love and a testament to His transformative work.

The transformational impact of shifting perspective in our faith life and view of God is a dynamic process that propels us toward a deeper, more meaningful relationship with our Creator. As we embrace a perspective rooted in trust, hope, gratitude, understanding, joy, empowerment, and intimacy, we uncover layers of spiritual growth and encounter God in ways we never thought possible. Through this transformative journey, we align our decisions, actions, and beliefs with His divine will, ultimately experiencing the fullness of life that comes from walking closely with our loving and sovereign Heavenly Father.

Perspective and Psychology

Like most things, there is a psychological perspective on the power of perspective, which can be explored in various branches of psychology. Let's delve into a few key aspects of this psychological viewpoint:

1. **Cognitive Psychology:** Cognitive psychology examines how our mental processes, including perception, attention, memory, and reasoning, influence our thoughts and behaviours. The concept of perspective plays a significant role in cognitive psychology, as it shapes how we interpret and make sense of the world around us. Our cognitive perspective can be influenced by our past experiences, beliefs, and emotions, leading to different interpretations of the same situation.

2. **Perceptual Bias:** Perceptual bias refers to the tendency of individuals to interpret sensory information based on their existing beliefs and expectations. This bias influences our perception of reality and can lead to discrepancies in how people interpret the same event. For example, two individuals with different perspectives may perceive a situation in contrasting ways, which can impact their emotional reactions and decision-making.

3. **Cognitive Distortions:** Cognitive distortions are irrational thought patterns that lead to skewed perceptions of reality. These distortions, such as black-and-white thinking,

overgeneralization, and catastrophizing, can greatly impact how we view ourselves, others, and situations. Shifting one's perspective by challenging and correcting these distortions is a central goal in cognitive-behavioural therapy.

4. **Positive Psychology**: Positive psychology emphasises the importance of cultivating a positive perspective to enhance well-being and personal growth. Adopting a positive perspective involves focusing on strengths, gratitude, and optimistic thinking. This approach encourages individuals to reframe challenges as opportunities for growth and to develop resilience in the face of adversity.

5. **Social Psychology:** Social psychology examines how social interactions and group dynamics influence individual behaviour and perception. The power of perspective is evident in phenomena like conformity, where individuals may adopt the perspective of a group to fit in or gain approval. Social psychology also explores how empathy and perspective-taking contribute to understanding others' emotions and motivations.

6. **Cultural Psychology:** Cultural psychology investigates how cultural norms, values, and experiences shape our perspectives and influence our behaviour. Different cultures may have distinct perspectives on concepts like time, individualism, and collectivism, leading

to variations in decision-making and communication styles.

7. **Mindfulness and Perspective Shift:** Mindfulness practices emphasise being present in the moment and observing thoughts and emotions without judgment. Mindfulness can lead to a shift in perspective by helping individuals detach from automatic and unhelpful thought patterns. This shift allows for greater awareness, self-regulation, and the ability to view situations from a more balanced and objective standpoint.

Incorporating these psychological insights into our understanding of perspective enriches our comprehension of how our thoughts, emotions, and beliefs influence our perception of the world. By becoming aware of our cognitive biases, cognitive distortions, and social influences, we can actively work to shift our perspective in ways that enhance our well-being, decision-making, and relationships.

The power of perspective is a crucial concept to consider from a psychological viewpoint, especially in the contemporary world. Considering the importance of mental health and well-being, the understanding one's own perspective and how it shapes their thoughts, emotions, and behaviours is central to mental health. Psychological interventions like cognitive-behavioural therapy (CBT) often involve helping individuals gain insight into their perspectives and beliefs to manage and improve their mental well-being. This improves one's interpersonal relationships where effective communication and healthy relationships rely on the ability to understand and appreciate the perspectives of others. In an age where digital communication is prevalent, misinterpretation and misunderstanding are common. A psychological perspective can help individuals navigate these challenges and build meaningful connections.

As the world becomes more interconnected through technology and globalisation, it's increasingly important to understand the perspectives of people from diverse cultural, ethnic, and socio-economic backgrounds. This is essential for international diplomacy, business relations, and collaborative problem-solving especially in the digital age, where information is readily available through various media channels and understanding different perspectives is crucial for media literacy. Psychological insights can help individuals critically evaluate information sources, recognise bias, and make informed judgments.

From a personal development standpoint, the ability to consider and integrate different perspectives can lead to greater self-awareness, personal growth, and a more fulfilling life. It can help individuals break out of rigid thinking patterns and expand their horizons.

In this day and age, where information flows rapidly, cultures intersect, and societal challenges are complex, the power of perspective is fundamental to addressing the many psychological, social, and ethical issues that arise. Psychological insights can provide valuable tools and strategies for individuals and society to navigate these challenges effectively and promote positive change.

Jesus used a lot of parables in order to engage the people with more than just their senses. He wanted our awareness to go deeper and for us to walk in revelation especially of the Kingdom. In Matthew 13:13, he answers and says, *"This is the reason I speak to the crowds in parables: because while [having the power of] seeing they do not see, and while [having the power of] hearing they do not hear, nor do they understand and grasp [spiritual things]."* This sentiment is also echoed in his conversations with his disciples in Mark 8:17-19 which states:

> Jesus, aware of this [discussion], said to them: *'Why are you discussing [the fact] that you have no bread? Do you still not see or understand? Are your hearts hardened? (18) Though you have eyes, do you not see? And though you have ears, do you not hear and listen [to what I have said]? And do you not remember...'*

Jesus's use of parables served a profound purpose in his teaching. He employed these stories to engage people on a deeper level, aiming to lead them towards a revelation of the Kingdom of God. His words in Matthew 13:13 emphasise the significance of this approach, highlighting that many could see and hear but not truly understand or grasp spiritual truths because of their perspectives. This theme is further underscored in his interactions with his disciples in Mark 8:17-19, where he challenges their perception and understanding. Ultimately, Jesus's use of parables was a powerful tool to encourage spiritual awakening and comprehension among his followers, urging them to see and hear with more profound insight, and this rings true especially in the days we are now living in.

8. THE POWER OF COMMUNICATION

The power of communication refers to the capacity to effectively convey messages, ideas, and information, lead conversations and interactions, regulate the flow of communication for clarity and understanding, and influence attitudes, behaviours, and decisions through persuasive and impactful expression. It encompasses the ability to convey thoughts clearly, listen actively, guide discussions, and shape perceptions through various mediums. By wielding this power, individuals can lead conversations, inspire change, regulate the exchange of information, and influence outcomes by skilfully communicating and connecting with others.

We cannot communicate effectively until we grasp language. When we think of language, we have to consider word choice, tone, and articulation. The power of language is remarkable in that it is a tool that shapes our thoughts, interactions, and the world around us. By exploring the nuances of word choice, tone, and articulation, we uncover how language can profoundly impact our relationships, decisions, and spiritual journey. The Bible, from the beginning, highlights God as a speaking being who was very careful with His word. When we read through, we begin to understand the very importance of us created as speaking beings in His image and why how we speak and what we say matters!

There is a weight to words. Words possess the extraordinary ability to build up or tear down, to inspire or discourage, and to convey truth or deception. Understanding the impact of word choice is crucial for aligning our language with our Christian values. The Bible emphasises the importance of guarding our speech and using words to edify and encourage (Ephesians 4:29). The tongue's power is compared to a small rudder that directs a great ship (James 3:4). Words can lead us toward righteousness or lead us astray, making intentional word choice essential.

Tone also bears significance especially when it comes to the emotional quality underlying our words. We can drastically alter their meaning and reception. Our tone reflects our attitudes and feelings, influencing how our message is perceived. Our tone can communicate care, empathy, and understanding. By adopting a gentle and compassionate tone, we reflect Christ's love in our interactions. Just as Jesus extended compassion to the hurting, our tone can offer solace to those in need. A misaligned tone can lead to misunderstandings. Choosing a tone of humility and respect fosters open communication and minimises potential conflicts.

Proverbs 15:1 reminds us that a gentle answer turns away wrath.

Effective articulation involves not only what we say, but also how we say it. Articulation encompasses clarity, confidence, and the manner in which we express our thoughts. Clear and concise articulation ensures our message is understood as intended. Just as Jesus communicated profound truths in simple parables, we can convey spiritual insights with clarity, enabling others to grasp the depth of our faith. Confident articulation stems from a firm foundation of faith. Boldly expressing our beliefs and values fosters an environment of authenticity and encourages others to engage in meaningful conversations.

The use of language holds profound implications for our spiritual growth, interactions, and alignment with God's will. Language is at the heart of our communication with God. Our prayers and praises reflect our reverence and intimacy with Him. Adopting a reverent tone and choosing words that honour God's greatness enriches our worship experience. Our language serves as a vehicle for sharing our faith. By articulating our personal testimonies and biblical truths, we can impact others and draw them closer to Christ. Thoughtful word choice and a humble tone contribute to effective evangelism.

The way we speak to ourselves internally influences our self-perception and mindset. Choosing words of self-compassion and affirmation aligns with God's view of us as His beloved children, fostering a positive self-concept.

The Divine Gift of Language:
The Revelation of the Power of Speech

God's creation of humanity as speaking beings reflects His intention for communication to be a cornerstone of our existence. Language is more than a tool; it's a divine gift that enables us to connect, understand, and express our innermost thoughts and emotions. Delving into this inherent aspect of our design sheds light on the profound role language plays in effective communication.

In the opening chapters of Genesis, God's creative act culminates with the formation of humanity, uniquely endowing us with the ability to communicate through language. This reflects His desire for relationship and dialogue with His creation. Language is a means through which we mirror God's nature of communication within the Trinity. Our capacity for language reflects the Imago Dei—the image of God—imprinted upon us. Just as God's word spoke the universe into existence, our words hold the power to shape and influence our reality. Our ability to communicate mirrors the Creator's divine power to bring forth order and meaning.

Language plays a pivotal role in the story of the Tower of Babel. The people at Babel are described as speaking "one language and one speech" (Genesis 11:1). This shared language facilitated their cooperation and coordination in building the tower. Language is not merely a tool for communication but also a means of conveying culture, knowledge, and identity. It is a fundamental aspect of human existence.

God's decision to confuse the people's language and scatter them across the Earth has been interpreted in various ways. One interpretation is that it was a divine response to human arrogance and hubris. The people at Babel were trying to elevate themselves to divine status, and in doing so, they were not humbly acknowledging their dependence on God. By dividing their languages and scattering them, God humbled them and reminded them of their limitations.

Another interpretation is that God's action was a way of promoting diversity and preventing a monolithic, centralised power. Had the people succeeded in building the tower, they might have concentrated immense power in one place, which could have been detrimental to human development and cooperation on a global scale. By dividing them into different language groups and scattering them, God encouraged cultural diversity and prevented a single, all-powerful entity from dominating.

The story of the Tower of Babel highlights the power of alliances and the significance of language in human endeavours. It also serves as a reminder of the importance of humility and diversity. By dividing the people through language, God's actions were not merely punitive but also had broader implications for the flourishing of humanity in all its diversity.

Throughout the Bible, God effectively communicates His will, promises, and truths to humanity through language. The Ten Commandments, the teachings of

Jesus, and the letters of Paul are all examples of divine communication conveyed through human language. Our ability to comprehend and respond to God's Word highlights the intricate connection between language and our spiritual journey.

Understanding the divine origin of language enhances our appreciation for effective communication, which encompasses both verbal and nonverbal aspects. Just as God's communication is clear and unambiguous, effective communication requires clarity in our verbal expression. Using precise words and structuring our sentences thoughtfully ensures that our message is received as intended. Nonverbal cues, such as body language, facial expressions, and tone of voice, play a significant role in effective communication. By aligning our nonverbal cues with our spoken words, we enhance understanding and authenticity in our interactions.

Just as God listens to our prayers with attentiveness, effective communication involves active listening. Engaging in active listening—being fully present and empathetically understanding others—fosters meaningful connections and demonstrates our genuine care. Language's power to influence and impact is evident throughout Scripture. Proverbs 18:21 states, "The tongue has the power of life and death." Our words hold the potential to inspire, comfort, and guide, or to hurt, discourage, and mislead. Choosing to use language to uplift and edify reflects our responsibility to steward this divine gift.

Language has the capacity to bridge divides and foster unity. Acts 2:6-8 portrays the miracle of Pentecost, where people of different languages were able to understand the disciples' message. Effective communication transcends cultural and linguistic barriers, creating connections that reflect God's desire for global reconciliation.

Language, we now see, was bestowed upon us as a divine gift, which mirrors God's desire for relationship, communication, and understanding. Just as God's Word brings life, our words carry the power to shape reality, impact hearts, and deepen connections. Through effective communication, we embody the divine intention for dialogue, reflecting the Creator's nature and contributing to the fulfilment of His redemptive plan. By embracing the sacredness of language and utilising it with purpose and grace, we engage in a transformative process that echoes God's design for connection and communion.

The Psychological and Sociological Significance of Communication and Language

Recognising the profound role of communication and language extends beyond the spiritual realm; it has significant implications in psychology and sociology, shedding light on the dynamics of human interaction, understanding, and societal cohesion.

Psychological Aspect:

Cognitive Development: Language plays a pivotal role in cognitive development, enabling children to organise their thoughts, express emotions, and grasp abstract concepts. Through language, individuals form mental representations of the world, enhancing problem-solving skills and critical thinking.

Emotional Expression: Language serves as a primary channel for emotional expression. Communicating feelings through words allows individuals to process and regulate emotions, contributing to psychological well-being. Effective emotional expression and communication can reduce stress and foster emotional resilience.

Identity and Self-Concept: Language enables the construction and expression of personal identity. The words we use to describe ourselves and our experiences contribute to our self-concept. Our language choices can reflect cultural, social, and individual identities, shaping how we perceive ourselves and how others perceive us.

Therapeutic Effect: In psychotherapy, communication serves as a therapeutic tool. Expressing thoughts and emotions in a safe environment promotes self-awareness and healing. Effective communication with therapists fosters understanding and insight, leading to personal growth and positive behavioural changes.

Sociological Aspect:

Social Cohesion: Effective communication is essential for building and maintaining social relationships and communities. Shared language allows individuals to connect, exchange ideas, and collaborate on common goals. Societies thrive when communication facilitates unity, cooperation, and the exchange of cultural values.

Norms and Socialisation: Language transmits societal norms, values, and cultural practices across generations. It shapes the process of socialisation, as individuals learn how to interact, behave, and think within their cultural context. Language perpetuates social norms and reinforces a sense of belonging.

Conflict Resolution: Communication skills are crucial for conflict resolution and negotiation. Effective communication helps individuals express grievances, reach compromises, and build understanding. Societies benefit from individuals who can engage in productive dialogue to address disagreements and maintain harmony.

Media and Influence: Language is a primary tool for media and communication platforms. Through language, media shapes public opinion, disseminates information, and influences collective behaviour. Societies are shaped by the language used in media, advertisements, and public discourse.

Cultural Diversity: Language reflects and perpetuates cultural diversity. Multilingual and multicultural societies benefit from linguistic diversity, which enriches cross-cultural understanding and fosters intergroup relationships. Effective communication across diverse languages enhances inclusivity and cultural exchange.

The psychological and sociological significance of communication and language is evident in their multifaceted roles in human development, interaction, and societal cohesion. Language shapes cognitive processes, emotional expression, and personal identity on a psychological level. Sociologically, communication fosters social cohesion, conveys cultural values, resolves conflicts, and influences societal dynamics. By understanding the intricate interplay of language and communication, we deepen our appreciation for their far-reaching impact on individual well-being, relationships, and the fabric of societies.

9. THE POWER OF RESTORATION

The power of restoration refers to the capacity to act in order to renew, repair, or recover something/one that has been damaged, depleted, or compromised. It involves leading efforts to revitalise or rehabilitate systems, relationships, environments, or well-being. This power includes the ability to regulate and guide processes that facilitate healing and recovery, while also influencing positive change and renewal. Through restoration, individuals or entities can act to bring about rejuvenation and improvement, leading to a sense of renewal and enhancement in various aspects of their lives and that of others.

The concept of restoration is a process that embodies God's redemptive nature and His ability to renew what was once broken or lost. Just as understanding enhances our vision, restoration rejuvenates our lives, relationships, and faith journey. Delving into the transformative power of restoration reveals its significance in our spiritual walk and personal growth.

God is the ultimate restorer and reveals His profound promise of renewal throughout Scripture. In the book of Joel, we find the assurance that God will restore what the locusts have eaten, reminding us that His divine grace can heal the wounds of time (Joel 2:25). The prophet Isaiah speaks of God as the one who comforts His people, bringing beauty from ashes and joy instead of mourning (Isaiah 61:3). The psalmist declares that the Lord is a shepherd who restores our souls, leading us beside still waters and paths of righteousness (Psalm 23:3-4). In the New Testament, we witness Jesus restoring sight to the blind (Luke 18:42), health to the sick (Mark 5:34), and hope to the lost (Luke 19:10). These verses remind us that God's nature is one of restoration, and through His love and power, He brings renewal and wholeness to our lives.

Restoration is a divine process of renewal and revival. It involves healing, rebuilding, and recovering what has been damaged or lost. Restoration heals wounds and renews our spiritual, emotional, and physical well-being. It addresses brokenness with the promise of restoration, just as God promises to bind up the broken-hearted (Isaiah 61:1).

The principle of restoration speaks to the heart of God's character and His desire to bring forth beauty from ashes. Restoration echoes God's redemptive plan. Through Christ's sacrifice, God offers restoration to humanity, reconciling us to Himself and offering a path to spiritual wholeness.

The birth of Jesus Christ stands as the ultimate testament to God's role as the restorer in the redemptive story of humanity. The Bible tells us that in sending His Son, God was not only bringing hope and salvation but also restoring a broken relationship between Himself and humanity. In the book of Genesis, sin entered the world through Adam and Eve, causing a rift between God and His creation. However, the birth of Jesus in Bethlehem marked the beginning of God's plan to restore that broken relationship.

Through the life, death, and resurrection of Jesus, God offered humanity forgiveness and redemption. The Apostle Paul emphasises this in Romans 5:18-19, stating that just as one man's disobedience (Adam) brought sin and death into the world, so one man's obedience (Jesus) brought righteousness and life. Jesus's birth initiated God's restorative mission, culminating in the cross, where our sins were paid for, and the empty tomb, where death was conquered.

Moreover, Jesus's ministry on Earth exemplified God's role as a restorer. He healed the sick, gave sight to the blind, and offered hope to the downtrodden. These acts of restoration mirrored God's desire to mend not only our spiritual relationship with Him but also to bring wholeness to our broken lives. The birth of Jesus was the beginning of God's grand plan of redemption and restoration for humanity. It serves as a powerful reminder that God is not only our Creator but also our Restorer, offering us the opportunity to experience renewal, reconciliation, and eternal life through faith in His Son, Jesus Christ.

The Process of Restoration

The journey of restoration involves several transformative stages:

Acknowledgment: Restoration begins with acknowledging the need for renewal. Just as the prodigal son recognized his need to return to his father's house, we must acknowledge areas of brokenness in our lives.

Repentance and Surrender: Repentance is a pivotal step in restoration. It involves turning away from destructive patterns and surrendering to God's healing work. Just as Peter was restored after denying Jesus, we experience restoration through genuine repentance.

Rebuilding and Renewal: Restoration involves rebuilding what was broken. Nehemiah's restoration of Jerusalem's walls serves as a powerful example of rebuilding and renewing that which was devastated.

The Bible contains numerous references to the concept of restoration, both in terms of God's restorative work and our responsibility to practice restoration within our relationships with others. Here are some key verses and insights:

Joel 2:25-26: *"I will restore to you the years that the swarming locust has eaten … You shall eat in plenty and be satisfied."*

Psalm 23:3: *"He restores my soul. He leads me in paths of righteousness for his name's sake."*

Psalm 51:12: *"Restore to me the joy of your salvation, and uphold me with a willing spirit."*

Galatians 6:1: *"Brothers, if anyone is caught in any transgression, you who are spiritual should restore him in a spirit of gentleness."*

Matthew 5:9: *"Blessed are the peacemakers, for they shall be called sons of God."*

Restoration and Relationships

Restoration extends to relationships, offering hope for reconciliation and healing. Restoration often requires forgiveness—releasing resentment and extending grace. Restoration is at the heart of the Gospel. God's redemptive plan through Christ is the ultimate act of restoration, reconciling humanity to Himself. Practicing restoration in relationships reflects Christ's example of reconciliation and forgiveness fostering unity and peace within relationships and communities. It involves resolving conflicts, forgiving offenses, and working towards reconciliation, aligning with Jesus's teaching to be peacemakers. Just as Joseph forgave his brothers, forgiveness paves the way for restored relationships. Restoration heals fractured relationships. The story of Jacob and Esau illustrates how God can mend broken bonds and reconcile estranged loved ones.

Restoration is woven into the fabric of our faith journey, for it ignites spiritual revival, breathing new life into our relationship with God. The Israelites' return to

God's ways after periods of disobedience reflects this cycle of revival and restoration.

As beings created in God's image, we are called to reflect His character. God is a restorer, and when we engage in restoration, we mirror His nature of redemption and renewal. Restoration heals emotional and relational wounds. Just as God heals our spiritual wounds, practicing restoration can lead to emotional healing, reconciliation, and the restoration of trust. It demonstrates love and compassion towards others. It involves extending grace, seeking understanding, and making efforts to mend broken relationships.

Restoring relationships testifies to the transformative power of God's grace. It shows that brokenness can be healed, conflicts can be resolved, and relationships can be redeemed through Christ's love and can contribute to emotional well-being. Unresolved conflicts and broken relationships can lead to emotional distress. Engaging in restoration brings relief, closure, and a sense of emotional restoration.

Restoration clarifies our purpose. Just as God restored the prophet Jeremiah's call, we discover renewed purpose through the process of restoration.

When we offer others restoration, it leads to powerful testimonies of God's faithfulness. Our stories of restoration inspire others and point them toward the hope of renewal. Restoration magnifies God's glory. Just as Lazarus's restoration from death displayed Jesus's power, our restoration showcases God's transformative work.

The power of restoration is a testament to God's boundless love and His desire to renew, heal, and transform.

Just as understanding enhances our vision, restoration revitalizes our lives, relationships, and faith. Through the process of restoration, we witness the miraculous renewal of what was once lost or broken, reflecting God's unwavering commitment to bring beauty, purpose, and wholeness out of the ashes of brokenness. Embracing the power of restoration allows us to experience the fullness of God's redemptive plan and become living testaments to His transformative grace.

The Psychology of Restoration

Psychologically, the concept of restoration in relation to well-being aligns closely with the idea of psychological recovery and resilience. Restoration refers to the process of recovering from stress, adversity, or challenges, and restoring a sense of balance, inner harmony, and overall well-being. This concept has several psychological implications:

1. Resilience and Adaptation:
Restoration in psychology often involves building resilience—the ability to bounce back from setbacks and maintain psychological well-being. It emphasises adaptive coping strategies that help individuals navigate challenges and recover their equilibrium.

2. Stress Reduction:
Restoration practices help regulate the body's stress response, promoting a state of calm and enhancing overall psychological well-being.

3. Psychological Recovery:

Restoration plays a crucial role in psychological recovery from trauma or difficult life events. It involves creating a supportive environment that promotes healing, helps process emotions, and gradually restores a sense of normalcy.

4. Self-Care and Well-Being:

Engaging in activities that promote self-care and relaxation contributes to restoration. Taking time to oneself, engaging in hobbies, and nurturing meaningful relationships all support psychological well-being.

5. Cognitive Restoration:

Restoration can also refer to cognitive restoration, which involves giving the mind a break from constant stimuli and allowing it to recover. This is essential for maintaining cognitive function, focus, and mental clarity.

6. Sleep and Restoration:

Adequate sleep is a critical aspect of psychological restoration. Sleep allows the brain to process emotions, consolidate memories, and recharge, contributing to overall well-being.

7. Environmental Restoration:

Being in nature or engaging with aesthetically pleasing environments contributes to psychological restoration. The phenomenon known as *"attention restoration theory"* suggests that natural settings can help rejuvenate mental resources.

8. Emotion Regulation:

Restoration practices often involve emotion regulation techniques. Developing skills to manage and regulate emotions helps individuals maintain psychological equilibrium and enhance their well-being.

9. Positive Psychology:

Positive psychology, a branch of psychology focused on well-being and flourishing, emphasizes activities that promote positive emotions, engagement, relationships, meaning, and accomplishment. These factors contribute to restoration and overall well-being.

Quintessentially, psychological restoration is closely linked to well-being through practices and strategies that help individuals recover, rejuvenate, and maintain a state of psychological health. It underscores the importance of proactive efforts to manage stress, promote resilience, and create an environment that supports mental and emotional restoration.

Practical Application of the Power of Restoration

Initiate Reconciliation: Take the initiative to reconcile with those you may have conflicts or misunderstandings with. Seek to mend relationships and restore harmony.

Practice Forgiveness: Choose to forgive others for their offenses, just as God forgives us. Forgiveness is a key component of restoration.

Seek Understanding: Strive to understand others' perspectives and emotions. This empathetic approach fosters open communication and paves the way for restoration.

Engage in Conflict Resolution: Address conflicts with a spirit of humility, patience, and a desire for resolution. Work together to find common ground and restore peace.

Extend Grace: Show grace and compassion towards those who have wronged you. Grace opens the door to healing and restoration.

Incorporating restoration into our relationships reflects God's redemptive plan and embodies the principles of love, forgiveness, and reconciliation. It contributes to healthier relationships, emotional well-being, and a more harmonious community, ultimately glorifying God through our actions.

Walking in a spirit of restoration is closely related to the principle of sowing and reaping in a profound and interconnected way. Both concepts hold valuable insights for our attitudes, actions, and relationships.

The principle of sowing and reaping is a biblical concept that accentuates the consequences of our actions. Just as a farmer sows seeds and later reaps a harvest, our choices and behaviours also yield outcomes either positive or negative. Walking in a spirit of restoration involves actively seeking to heal, mend, and reconcile broken relationships, fostering harmony and unity. It requires extending forgiveness, showing empathy, and making efforts to restore what has been damaged.

The relationship between these concepts lies in the outcomes we reap based on our approach to restoration; for when we sow seeds of restoration we actively work towards healing and reconciling relationships and we are sowing seeds of love, forgiveness, and empathy. Just as sowing good seeds in a field leads to a bountiful harvest, sowing seeds of restoration yields positive results. Reaping the benefits of restored relationships, emotional healing, and unity contributes to a healthier and more fulfilling life. Conversely, if we neglect restoration and allow bitterness, conflict, and brokenness to persist, we are sowing negative seeds. The consequences of this neglect may include strained relationships, emotional distress, and a lack of peace. The principles of sowing and reaping and walking in a spirit of restoration align with various biblical teachings:

Galatians 6:7-9: *"Do not be deceived: God is not mocked, for whatever one sows, that will he also reap."*

Matthew 5:9: *"Blessed are the peacemakers, for they shall be called sons of God."*

Experiencing the positive effects of restoration inspires us to continue sowing good seeds in our relationships, perpetuating a cycle of healing, growth, and transformation.

Walking in a spirit of restoration aligns with the principle of sowing and reaping by encouraging us to sow seeds of love, forgiveness, and reconciliation in our interactions with others. The positive reaping of restored relationships and emotional healing underscores the importance of embracing restoration as a key aspect of our attitudes and actions. By intertwining these concepts, we participate in a redemptive process that mirrors God's character and plan for restoration and renewal.

Restoration, whether in a physical or spiritual context, shares underlying principles of renewal, healing, and transformation. The application and focus of spiritual restoration includes reconnecting with God and aligning one's life with divine principles. It's about returning to a state of spiritual intimacy and closeness with the Creator.

Spiritual restoration can lead to a renewed sense of purpose and calling. It involves discovering God's plan for one's life and aligning one's actions with His will.

While physical restoration focuses on repairing external, tangible elements, spiritual restoration pertains to inner healing and alignment with divine values.

Ultimately, whether in the physical or spiritual realm, restoration embodies the concept of renewal, healing, and bringing forth beauty from brokenness. It reflects the belief in the potential for transformation and the power to restore what was lost or damaged.

EPILOGUE:
LIVING IN POWER

Now that you have read the power pillars, it is imperative to put them in practice by living in power through God's grace and authority. Living in power begins with a deep understanding and acceptance of God's unmerited favour, also known as grace. This grace empowers us to overcome challenges, grow spiritually, and tap into our fullest potential. By recognising that we are recipients of this divine grace, we shed feelings of inadequacy and step into our identity as empowered individuals.

God's authority, an extension of His sovereignty, provides us with a roadmap for living purposefully and responsibly. By aligning our actions and decisions with His divine principles, we position ourselves to influence our surroundings positively. This authority is not domineering; rather, it guides us towards making choices that reflect wisdom, compassion, and love.

Living in power is not a passive state but an active one. When we yield to God's grace and authority, we are propelled to act with purpose. This entails using our capacities to create meaningful change in our lives and the lives of others. Through leadership grounded in humility and empathy, we set an example that inspires those around us.

A critical aspect of living in power is the ability to regulate our inner world. God's grace empowers us to exercise self-control over our thoughts, emotions, and behaviours. By nurturing a disciplined mindset, we guard against negative influences and destructive patterns. This self-regulation ensures that our actions are aligned with our values and the authority bestowed upon us.

Living in power is not confined to personal growth; it extends to the realm of influence. As we walk in God's grace and authority, our actions radiate positivity and attract others towards the light. Through our interactions, we can inspire, motivate, and uplift, creating a ripple effect that extends far beyond our immediate circle.

The journey of living in power through God's grace and authority is not a destination but a continuous evolution. It requires a willingness to learn, adapt, and remain steadfast in our faith. As we navigate life's challenges with the conviction that we are empowered by divine grace and guided by divine authority, we experience a profound transformation that elevates both our individual lives and the world around us.

Embracing God's Grace: A Foundation for Power

Ephesians 2:8-9 - *"For by grace you have been saved through faith. And this is not your own doing; it is the gift of God, not a result of works, so that no one may boast."*

Acknowledging Divine Authority: Navigating Life's Path

Proverbs 3:5-6 - *"Trust in the LORD with all your heart, and do not lean on your own understanding. In all your ways acknowledge him, and he will make straight your paths."*

Acting with Purpose: Empowerment in Action

1 Timothy 4:12 - *"Let no one despise you for your youth, but set the believers an example in speech, in conduct, in love, in faith, in purity."*

Regulating Our Inner World: Mastering Self-Control

Galatians 5:22-23 - *"But the fruit of the Spirit is love, joy, peace, forbearance, kindness, goodness, faithfulness, gentleness and self-control."*

Influencing Others: A Ripple Effect

Matthew 5:16 - *"In the same way, let your light shine before others, so that they may see your good works and give glory to your Father who is in heaven."*

Living in Power: A Lifelong Journey

Philippians 1:6 - *"And I am sure of this, that he who began a good work in you will bring it to completion at the day of Jesus Christ."*

In conclusion, living in power through God's grace and authority is a transformative endeavour that empowers us to act, lead, regulate, and influence in ways that align with divine principles. Embracing this paradigm shift allows us to live purposefully, make a positive impact, and contribute to the betterment of humanity.

The word remains our foundation as we begin to apply the principles in this book to affect change in our lives and that of others. Remember, it is in His image that you were created and He lives in you through His Holy Spirit. Be not ashamed nor afraid but step out in faith knowing that God has given you power, the ability to live well and experience the best He has for you both in the natural and the spiritual!

REVIEW REQUESTED:

We'd like to know if you enjoyed the book. Please consider leaving a review on the platform from which you purchased the book.

Milton Keynes UK
Ingram Content Group UK Ltd.
UKHW030824010824
446326UK00001B/5

9 781682 353714